SLOVENIA TRAVEL GUIDE BOOK 2023

Experience the Beauty and Adventure of Slovenia in 2023 and beyond

Kian Wright

DISCLAIMER

This book is a work of fiction. Names, characters, places, and incidents either are the product of the author's imagination or are used fictitiously. Any resemblance to actual persons, living or dead, events, or locales is entirely coincidental.

Copyright © 2023 by Kian Wright

All rights reserved. No part of this book may be reproduced, scanned, or distributed in any printed or electronic form without permission. Please do not participate in or encourage piracy of copyrighted materials in violation of the author's rights. Purchase only authorized editions.

This book is licensed for your enjoyment only. It may not be re-sold or given away to other people. If you would like to share this book with another person, please purchase an additional copy for each recipient. If you're reading this book and did not purchase it, or it was not purchased for your use only, then please return it to your favourite bookseller and purchase your copy. Thank you for respecting the hard work of this author.

This book is published by Kian Wright, and all rights are reserved by the publisher.

Disclaimer

The information contained in this book is for general information purposes only.

The information is provided by the author and while we endeavour to keep the information up to date and correct, we make no representations or warranties of any kind, express or implied, about the completeness, accuracy, reliability, suitability, or availability concerning the book or the information, products, services, or related graphics contained in the book for any purpose. Any reliance you place on such information is therefore strictly at your own risk. In no event will the author or publisher be liable for any loss or damage including without limitation, indirect or consequential loss or damage, or any loss or damage whatsoever arising from loss of data or profits arising out of, or in connection with, the use of this Book.

Please note that this disclaimer is subject to change without notice.

TABLE OF CONTENT

INTRODUCTION

Introduction to Slovenia

Planning Your Trip to Slovenia

Best Time to Visit Slovenia

Maps and directions to make your stay in Slovenia easy and explore like a local

Getting to Slovenia

Transportation within Slovenia

Possible itinerary options to explore Slovenia like a local

Accommodations in Slovenia

Must-See Attractions in Slovenia

Off the Beaten Path: Hidden Gems in Slovenia

Experiencing the Local Culture in Slovenia

Outdoor Activities in Slovenia

Museums and galleries in Slovenia

Food and Drink in Slovenia

Campsites in Slovenia that offer facilities for RVs

Shopping in Slovenia

Health and Safety in Slovenia

Tips for Traveling in Slovenia on a Budget

Conclusion: Making the Most of Your Trip to Slovenia

INTRODUCTION

Welcome to Slovenia, one of the most beautiful and diverse countries in Europe! With its stunning natural scenery, rich cultural heritage, and charming towns and cities, Slovenia is an ideal destination for anyone looking for a unique travel experience.

Whether you're a first-time visitor or a seasoned traveller, the Slovenia Travel Guide Book 2023 will help you plan and enjoy your trip to this fascinating country.

This comprehensive guidebook provides detailed information on everything you need to know before and during your trip to Slovenia. From the best time to visit and how to get there, to accommodations, transportation, and must-see attractions, we've got you covered. We'll also introduce you to some hidden gems and off-the-beaten-path destinations that are sure to delight you.

In addition to practical travel information, this guidebook also explores Slovenia's rich culture, history, possible itinerary, maps and directions, cuisine and many more.

You'll learn about the country's traditions and festivals, as well as its thriving arts and music scene. And of course, we'll also give you tips on where to find the best food and drink, as well as the best places to shop for local crafts and souvenirs.

Whether you're looking for adventure, relaxation, or a bit of both, Slovenia has something for everyone. So sit back, relax, and let the Slovenia Travel Guide

Book 2023 be your guide to this enchanting country.

Introduction to Slovenia

Located in Central Europe, Slovenia is a small but incredibly diverse country that is often overlooked by tourists.

Bordered by Italy to the west, Austria to the north, Hungary to the northeast, and Croatia to the south and southeast, Slovenia is an ideal destination for travellers who want to experience a little bit of everything.

Slovenia has a rich history and culture that dates back thousands of years. The country's landscape is dotted with ancient castles, churches, and other historic landmarks, many of which are still standing today. The Slovenian people are proud of their heritage and have worked hard to preserve their traditions and way of life.

One of the things that makes Slovenia so unique is its natural beauty. The country is home to stunning mountains, sparkling lakes, and picturesque forests that are perfect for hiking, skiing, and other outdoor activities. The Julian Alps, located in the northwest of the country, offer some of the most breathtaking views in all of Europe.

Slovenia is also known for its delicious cuisine, which is a blend of Mediterranean, Austrian, and Hungarian influences. Some of the country's most famous dishes include potica (a sweet bread), jota (a stew made with beans and sauerkraut), and štruklji (a type of dumpling).

Whether you're interested in history, culture, nature, or food, Slovenia has something to offer. In the following chapters, we'll delve deeper into the country's many attractions and help you plan your perfect Slovenian vacation.

Planning Your Trip to Slovenia

Slovenia is a stunning nation with a variety of landscapes, including the Alpine Mountains, the Adriatic Sea, and numerous little cities and towns in between.

The following advice will help you plan your trip to Slovenia:

1. Decide when you'll be travelling:

Although you can travel to Slovenia any time of year, the ideal time to go will depend on your interests. Winter is best for skiing and other winter sports, while summer is best for visiting the seaside and engaging in outdoor activities.

2. Choose your location:

Despite Slovenia's modest size, there is a lot to see and do there. The capital city of Ljubljana is a must-see, but the

Julian Alps, the Karst area, and the seaside resort of Piran are also well-liked vacation spots.

3. Make hotel reservations:

Slovenia offers a wide range of lodging alternatives, from high-end hotels to inexpensive hostels. Make sure to reserve early, especially during the busiest season.

4. Make your travel arrangements:

The public transport system in Slovenia is highly developed and includes rental automobiles, trains and buses. Consider getting an Urbana card in Ljubljana if you intend to use public transport for quick access to buses.

5. Pack appropriately:

Pack for the season you'll be travelling since Slovenia has a temperate climate. Make sure you have the right equipment with you if you intend to engage in any outdoor activities.

6. Investigate the culture:

It is important to familiarise yourself with Slovenian culture before visiting. Although Slovenes are warm and welcoming, it is still important to respect regional traditions and customs.

7. Test the food and beverage:

Slovenian cuisine has its distinctive specialities in addition to being inspired by its neighbours. Make sure to sample some of the regional specialities, including evapii (grilled minced meat) and the traditional pastry potica.

8. Take advantage of nature:

Spend some time outdoors exploring because Slovenia is recognised for its stunning scenery. There is something for everyone, from bathing in the sea to mountain trekking.

9. Be careful:

Even though Slovenia is generally a safe country, vigilance should still be exercised. Keep your possessions safe, and pay attention to your surroundings, especially in crowded places.

10. Having fun:

Enjoy your trip and see everything Slovenia has to offer—it's a great place to visit!

Consider joining a guided tour if you want to make the most of your visit to Slovenia and discover more about its history and culture. There are several choices, including adventure trips, wine-tasting tours, and city strolling tours.

11. Learn the following Slovene phrases:

Slovenes can communicate in a variety of languages, including English, but learning a few phrases in Slovenian can help you connect with the populace and demonstrate your interest in their way of life.

12. Buying mementoes:

Slovenia offers a wide variety of distinctive souvenirs, including handcrafted items, vintage apparel, and regional foods. Spend some time perusing the neighbourhood markets and shops to discover the ideal memento to cherish as a reminder of your vacation.

Finally, organising a trip to Slovenia can be fun This advice. This advice will help you get the most out of your time in this stunning nation, immerse yourself in the culture, and make lifelong memories. Slovenia has something to offer for everyone, whether you're visiting the cities, taking in the outdoors, or sampling the local food. So prepare for the trip of a lifetime to Slovenia by packing your bags!

Best Time to Visit Slovenia

Slovenia is a beautiful country that has something to offer all year round. The best time to visit Slovenia depends on what you want to do and see during your trip.

Here's a more detailed explanation of each season in Slovenia, along with some things travellers can see and enjoy:

Summer (June-August):

Summer is the busiest time to visit Slovenia, with warm weather and plenty of outdoor activities to enjoy.

Some popular things to see and do during the summer months include:

Visit Lake Bled: One of Slovenia's most iconic destinations, Lake Bled is a stunningly beautiful alpine lake with a small island in the middle. Visitors can take a traditional pletna boat ride to the island, climb up to the castle for views of the lake, or simply relax on the lakeshore.

Explore Triglav National Park: Slovenia's only national park is a paradise for outdoor enthusiasts, with hiking trails, cycling routes, and stunning mountain scenery. Some popular hikes include the Vintgar Gorge, the Soca River Trail, and the Seven Lakes Valley.

Enjoy the coast: Slovenia has a small but lovely stretch of coastline along the Adriatic Sea, with towns like Piran and Portoroz offering beaches, seafood restaurants, and historic architecture.

Attend a festival: Summer is festival season in Slovenia, with events like the Ljubljana Jazz Festival, the Ana Desetnica street theatre festival, and the Pivo in Cvetje beer and flower festival taking place throughout the season.

Spring (March-May):

Spring is a great time to visit Slovenia if you want to avoid the summer crowds and enjoy the blooming wildflowers.

Some popular things to see and do during the spring months include:

Visit the Postojna Cave: One of Slovenia's most popular attractions, the Postojna Cave is a vast underground network of caverns and tunnels that visitors can explore on a guided tour. The cave is home to a variety of unique creatures, including the proteus salamander.

Go wine tasting: Slovenia has a long history of winemaking, and the spring months are a great time to visit the country's vineyards and taste some of the local varietals.

Explore Ljubljana: Slovenia's capital city is a charming destination with a pedestrian-friendly old town, a castle perched on a hilltop, and plenty of museums and galleries to explore.

Visit the Skocjan Caves: Another spectacular cave system, the Skocjan Caves are a UNESCO World Heritage Site with underground rivers, canyons, and waterfalls.

Fall (September-November):

Fall is a beautiful time to visit Slovenia, with the changing colours of the leaves creating a picturesque landscape.

Some popular things to see and do during the fall months include:

Go mushroom hunting: Slovenia is home to a variety of edible mushrooms, and the fall months are a great time to forage for them in the forests.

Visit the wine regions: As mentioned earlier, fall is the harvest season for Slovenia's winemakers, making it an ideal time to visit the country's vineyards and taste the new vintages.

Attend a harvest festival: Many towns and villages in Slovenia celebrate the harvest season with festivals, fairs, and markets, offering visitors a chance to sample local foods and drinks and experience traditional music and dance.

Take a scenic train ride: Slovenia has several picturesque train routes that offer stunning views of the country's mountains, valleys, and forests.

Winter (December-February):

Slovenia's winter months can be cold and snowy, but they also offer some unique opportunities for travellers.

Some popular things to see and do during the winter months include:

Go skiing:

Slovenia has several ski resorts, including Kranjska Gora, Vogel, and Krvavec, that offer a variety of runs for skiers and snowboarders of all levels of experience.

Visit the Christmas markets:

Slovenia's cities and towns come alive during the holiday season with festive Christmas markets. The market in Ljubljana is particularly popular, with vendors selling traditional crafts, food, and drink.

Explore the underground caves:

The winter months are a great time to visit Slovenia's underground caves, as they offer a respite from the cold temperatures outside. The Postojna Cave and Skocjan Caves are open year-round and offer guided tours.

Try ice climbing:

Slovenia's Julian Alps offer a variety of ice climbing routes for experienced climbers. Some popular spots include the frozen waterfalls of Mlačca and Peričnik.

Overall, Slovenia is a year-round destination with something to offer in every season. Whether you're interested in outdoor activities, culture and history, food and drink, or simply enjoying the beautiful scenery, there's plenty to see and do in this small but vibrant country.

Maps and directions to make your stay in Slovenia easy and explore like a local

Slovenia is a beautiful country with many interesting sights to see and things to do.

Here are some general tips for travellers and tourists visiting Slovenia:

Getting around: Slovenia is a small country, so getting around is relatively easy. The most common modes of transportation are by car, bus or train. Car rental companies can be found at the major airports, and buses and trains run frequently between the major cities.

Language: Slovenian is the official language of Slovenia, but many people also speak English, German, and Italian. It's always a good idea to learn a few basic phrases in Slovenian before you go, as it can be helpful when communicating with locals.

Currency: The official currency of Slovenia is the Euro (€). ATMs are widely available throughout the country, and credit cards are accepted in most places.

Maps and directions: Google Maps is a great resource for navigating Slovenia. You can download offline maps in advance and use them to navigate without an internet connection. You can also use the Google Maps app to search for nearby attractions, restaurants, and hotels(details on this are provided below)

Must-see attractions: Some of the top attractions in Slovenia include Lake Bled, the capital city of Ljubljana, the Postojna Cave system, the Skocjan Caves, and the medieval town of Piran on the coast.

Food and drink: Slovenia has a rich culinary tradition, with many delicious dishes to try. Local specialities include cevapcici (grilled meat), idrijski zlikrofi (dumplings stuffed with potato and bacon), and potica (a sweet bread filled with nuts or other fillings). Slovenia is also known for its excellent wines, especially white wines like Sauvignon Blanc and Chardonnay.

Safety: Slovenia is a safe country with a low crime rate, but it's always a good idea to take basic safety precautions, such as keeping your valuables secure and being aware of your surroundings.

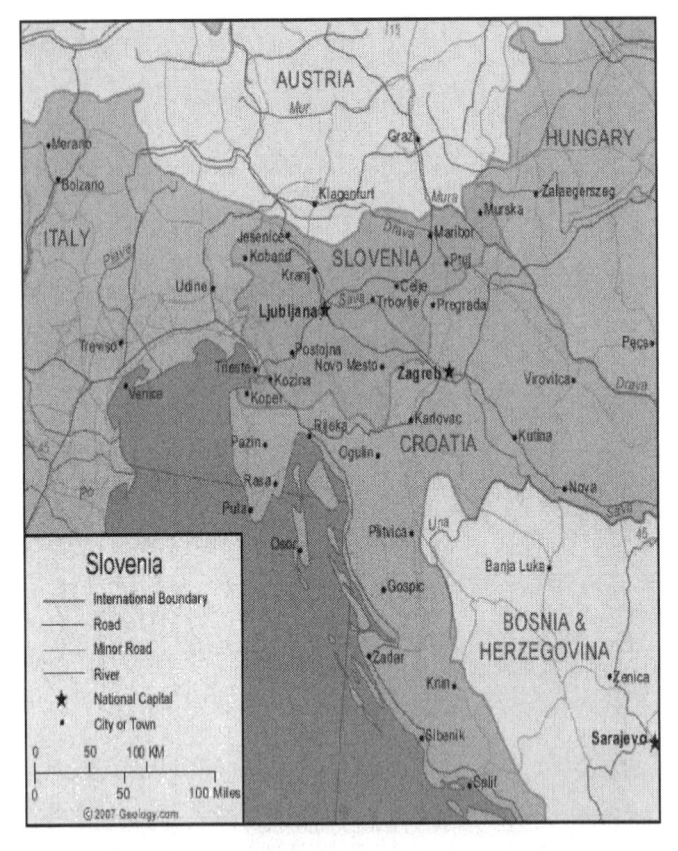

Credit: Geology.com

Some different options for finding maps of Slovenia in case the above map is not helpful:

Online map services: Google Maps and Bing Maps both offer detailed maps of Slovenia, which you can access from your computer or smartphone. They also provide directions and the ability to search for nearby businesses and attractions.

Paper maps: If you prefer a physical map, you can purchase a paper map of Slovenia at most bookstores, travel agencies, or gas stations. Many of these maps will also include information about local attractions and accommodations.

Tourist information centres: You can also visit a local tourist information centre, where you can pick up maps and brochures about the region. These centres are typically located in major cities and tourist destinations.

GPS devices: If you're renting a car, your rental company may offer GPS devices that come preloaded with maps of Slovenia. This can be a convenient way to navigate the country without relying on your phone or a paper map.

Mobile apps: There are several mobile apps available that provide maps of Slovenia, including Maps.Me, OsmAnd, and HERE WeGo. These apps can be downloaded to your smartphone and used offline, which can be helpful if you don't have access to Wi-Fi or cellular data.

I hope this helps you find the maps you need to navigate Slovenia!

Getting to Slovenia

Getting to Slovenia as a traveller or tourist can be done by various means of transportation.

Here are some options:

By Plane: Slovenia has a few international airports, including the Ljubljana Jože Pučnik Airport, which is the country's main airport. It is located 26 km from Ljubljana, the capital city, and serves several European cities. Another option is the Maribor Edvard Rusjan Airport, which serves a few destinations in Europe.

By Train: Slovenia is well connected by train to its neighbouring countries and some other European destinations. The main train station in Ljubljana offers connections to several European cities, including Vienna, Budapest, Munich, and Venice.

By Bus: Buses are a common way to travel within Slovenia and to other

European countries. The main bus station in Ljubljana offers connections to several European cities, including Zagreb, Vienna, and Munich.

By Car: Slovenia is well connected by highways to its neighbouring countries. The most common entry points by car are from Austria, Italy, and Croatia.

By Boat: Slovenia has a small port in Koper, which is located on the coast. There are ferry connections to Venice, Italy, and to some Croatian cities.

Regardless of how you choose to get to Slovenia, make sure to check the latest travel information and entry requirements, especially regarding COVID-19 restrictions.

Slovenia is a small country located in central Europe, bordering Italy, Austria, Hungary, and Croatia. Despite its small size, Slovenia is a popular destination for tourists due to its beautiful scenery, rich cultural heritage, and outdoor activities such as hiking and skiing.

Here's a more detailed explanation of how to get to Slovenia from different parts of the world:

From Europe: Traveling to Slovenia from other European countries is relatively easy. Several low-cost airlines offer flights to Slovenia, including Wizz Air, EasyJet, and Ryanair. These airlines connect Slovenia with cities such as London, Paris, Amsterdam, Berlin, and Barcelona. Additionally, there are regular train and bus connections from neighbouring countries such as Austria, Italy, and Croatia.

From North America: There are no direct flights from North America to Slovenia, but several airlines offer connecting flights through major European airports such as Frankfurt, Munich, or Vienna. Alternatively, travellers can fly to nearby airports such as Venice, Italy or Zagreb, Croatia, and then take a train, bus, or rental car to Slovenia.

From Asia: There are no direct flights from Asia to Slovenia, but several airlines offer connecting flights through major European airports such as Amsterdam, Frankfurt, or Istanbul. Alternatively, travellers can fly to nearby airports such as Vienna or Munich, and then take a train or bus to Slovenia.

From Australia and New Zealand: There are no direct flights from Australia or New Zealand to Slovenia, but several airlines offer connecting flights through major European airports such as London, Paris, or Frankfurt. Alternatively, travellers can fly to nearby airports such as Venice or Zagreb, and then take a train or bus to Slovenia.

Overall, travelling to Slovenia from anywhere in the world is relatively easy, with several options for transportation available. As always, travellers should check the latest entry requirements and COVID-19 restrictions before making their travel plans.

Transportation within Slovenia

Slovenia has a well-established transport system that makes getting across the nation simple for visitors and travellers.

Here are a few of the available modes of transportation:

Bus:

The bus is the most popular method of transportation in Slovenia, and it connects all of the country's major cities and towns regularly. At the bus stations, you can look up the schedule and purchase tickets, or you can use online resources like FlixBus, Nomago, and Arriva.

Train:

The capital city of Ljubljana is connected by railroads to other significant cities around Slovenia as well as to nearby nations including Croatia, Austria, and Italy. At the train stations, you can look up the schedule and purchase tickets, or you can use internet resources like Slovenske Venice.

Car:

Renting a car in Slovenia is an option if you like to drive. You may reserve a car online or at the airport, and several well-known car rental firms, including Hertz, Europcar, and Sixt, have locations in the nation.

Taxi:

In the majority of Slovenia's towns and cities, taxis are available. In contrast to other forms of transportation, they can be rather pricey, particularly over longer distances.

Cycling:

Cycling is very popular in Slovenia, where there are numerous scenic routes and trails. You can either take a guided bike tour or rent a bike from one of the many bike rental businesses in Ljubljana and neighbouring cities.

Walking:

Since Slovenia is a small nation, many major cities and tourist destinations are accessible on foot. Travelling on foot is a great way to see the country and find hidden jewels that you may otherwise miss if you take a bus or a car.

Overall, Slovenia has a range of transit choices for visitors, making it simple to go around and take in all the sights.

Several variables, including the distance travelled, the hour of the day, and the season, can affect how much different modes of transportation cost in Slovenia.

Here are some rough costs for each type of transportation mentioned:

Bus:

In Slovenia, bus fares are reasonably priced. A single ticket can cost between €1.5 and €2 for a short trip (up to 10 km), and between €4 and €7 for a longer travel (up to 50 km). A prepaid card might help you save money by offering a 20% discount on ordinary fares.

Train:

In Slovenia, train tickets are comparable to bus fares. A single ticket for a short trip may cost between €2 and €3, while a longer trip may cost between €6 and €15. Once more, you can save money by buying a prepaid card or making reservations in advance.

Car:

In Slovenia, renting a car may get pricey, especially in the summer. The type of car, the length of the rental, and the location all affect the cost. A modest automobile will typically cost between €40 and €60 per day, whereas a premium car might cost up to €100.

Taxi:

In Slovenia, taxis are somewhat pricey in comparison to other modes of transportation. While a longer trip may cost between €50 and €100, a short ride within the city centre may cost between €5.00 and €10.00.

Cycling:

Slovenia is a somewhat inexpensive place to rent a bike. For about €15–€20.00 per day, you can rent a bike; costs drop for longer rentals. The cost of a guided bike tour can range from €40.00 to €80.00 per person.

Walking:

Walking is the most economical method of transportation in Slovenia because it is free. However, some tourist destinations and attractions may charge admission.

Slovenia provides a variety of transit choices to accommodate various needs and tastes. To discover the greatest value for your travel needs, it's critical to study prices and evaluate several possibilities.

Possible itinerary options to explore Slovenia like a local

Slovenia is a beautiful country in Central Europe that offers a unique blend of natural beauty, historical landmarks, and cultural experiences.

Here are three different itinerary options for exploring Slovenia, based on the length of your trip:

3-DAY ITINERARY:

Day 1: Ljubljana and Lake Bled

Ljubljana

Lake Bled

- Explore the historic city centre of Ljubljana, taking in the famous

Triple Bridge, the Ljubljana Castle, and the Central Market

- Head to Lake Bled and take a boat ride to the island in the middle of the lake

- Climb up to the Bled Castle for a stunning view of the lake and surrounding mountains

- Enjoy a traditional cream cake (Cremona retina) before heading back to Ljubljana

Day 2: Piran and the Slovenian Coast

- Visit the charming seaside town of Piran on the Adriatic Sea

- Walk along the narrow streets and admire the Venetian architecture

- Enjoy fresh seafood for lunch and take a dip in the sea

- End the day with a visit to the nearby Portorož and its many spa centres

Day 3: Škocjan Caves and the Karst Region

- Visit the Škocjan Caves, a UNESCO World Heritage Site known for their stunning natural beauty

- Take a tour of the Lipica Stud Farm, home to the famous Lipizzaner horses

- End your trip with a visit to the town of Divača, where you can enjoy a traditional Karst meal before heading back to Ljubljana

7-DAY ITINERARY:

Days 1-3: Ljubljana, Lake Bled, and the Julian Alps

- Spend the first few days in Ljubljana and Lake Bled, as described in the 3-day itinerary

- Take a day trip to the Soča Valley and the Julian Alps, exploring the emerald Soča River, white-water rafting, and hiking in the mountains

Days 4-5: Wine Region and Ptuj

- Visit Maribor, the centre of the wine region, and take a tour of the Old Vine House

- Enjoy a wine tasting and sample some of the local cuisines

- Spend a day in the town of Ptuj, exploring the medieval castle, the old town, and the famous Ptuj Thermal Spa

Days 6-7: Coastal Towns and the Karst Region

- Spend a day in Piran and Portorož, enjoying the sea, the fresh seafood, and the spa centres

- Visit the Škocjan Caves, Lipica Stud Farm, and the town of Divača, as described in the 3-day itinerary

10-DAY ITINERARY:

Days 1-3: Ljubljana, Lake Bled, and the Julian Alps

- Spend the first few days in Ljubljana and Lake Bled, as described in the 3-day itinerary

- Take a day trip to the Soča Valley and the Julian Alps, exploring the emerald Soča River, white-water rafting, and hiking in the mountains

Days 4-5: Wine Region and Ptuj

- Visit Maribor, the centre of the wine region, and take a tour of the Old Vine House

- Enjoy a wine tasting and sample some of the local cuisines
- Spend a day in the town of Ptuj, exploring the medieval castle, the

old town, and the famous Ptuj Thermal Spa

Days 6-7: Coastal Towns and the Karst Region

- Spend a day in Piran and Portorož, enjoying the sea, the fresh seafood, and the spa centres

- Visit the Škocjan Caves, Lip

Days 8-9: Triglav National Park and Lake Bohinj

- Visit Triglav National Park and explore the stunning natural beauty of the park, including the Vintgar Gorge, the Tolmin Gorges, and the Kozjak Waterfall

- Spend a day at Lake Bohinj, where you can hike, swim, and relax on the shores of one of Slovenia's most beautiful lakes

Day 10: Postojna Cave and Predjama Castle

- Visit the Postojna Cave, one of Slovenia's most famous attractions, with its incredible underground formations and unique fauna

- Explore the nearby Predjama Castle, built into the side of a cliff and surrounded by beautiful countryside

- End your trip with a final night in Ljubljana, where you can enjoy a farewell dinner and take in the city's lively nightlife.

Conclusion

Slovenia is a beautiful country with a variety of attractions and experiences to offer travellers and tourists. Whether you have 3 days, 7 days, or 10 days, you can plan an itinerary that allows you to explore the best of what Slovenia has to offer.

Some of the must-see attractions include the historic city centre of Ljubljana, the stunning Lake Bled and its castle, the charming coastal town of

Piran, the beautiful Julian Alps and Triglav National Park, the wine region around Maribor, and the famous Postojna Cave and Predjama Castle.

In addition to its natural beauty, Slovenia offers a rich culture, delicious cuisine, and friendly locals. Exploring Slovenia like a local will give you a deeper appreciation for this hidden gem of a country in the heart of Europe.

Before we move to the next step let's quickly go through the necessary information you need to know for each location mentioned above. Which are;

Ljubljana:

Address: Ljubljana, Slovenia
Currency: Euro (EUR)
Language: Slovenian, but many people also speak English
Must-see attractions: Triple Bridge, Ljubljana Castle, Central Market, Dragon Bridge, Tivoli Park, National Gallery of Slovenia, Metelkova Mesto (alternative culture centre)

Lake Bled:

Address: Bled, Slovenia
Currency: Euro (EUR)
Language: Slovenian, but many people also speak English

Must-see attractions: Bled Castle, Island on Lake Bled, Vintgar Gorge, Blejski Vintgar Trail, Mala Osojnica Hill, Bled Cream Cake (Kremna Rezina)

Piran:

Address: Piran, Slovenia
Currency: Euro (EUR)
Language: Slovenian, but many people also speak Italian and English

Must-see attractions: Tartini Square, St. George's Parish Church, Walls of Piran, Aquarium Piran, Fiesa Lake, Strunjan Nature Reserve

Portorož:

Address: Portorož, Slovenia
Currency: Euro (EUR)
Language: Slovenian, but many people also speak Italian and English

Must-see attractions: Portorož Beach, Tartini Square, Church of St. Bernardin, Piran Salt Pans, Forma Viva

Škocjan Caves:

Address: Matavun, Slovenia
Currency: Euro (EUR)
Language: Slovenian, but many people also speak English
Must-see attractions: Škocjan Caves Park, Velika Dolina, Mala Dolina, Rimstone Pools, Cerkvenik Bridge, Škocjan Education Trail

Lipica Stud Farm:

Address: Lipica, Slovenia
Currency: Euro (EUR)
Language: Slovenian, but many people also speak English

Must-see attractions: Lipica Stud Farm, Lipizzaner Horses, Lipica Golf Club, Lipica Park

Maribor:

Address: Maribor, Slovenia
Currency: Euro (EUR)
Language: Slovenian, but many people also speak English
Must-see attractions: Old Vine House, Maribor Castle, Maribor Regional Museum, Maribor City Park, Lent Promenade

Ptuj:

Address: Ptuj, Slovenia
Currency: Euro (EUR)
Language: Slovenian, but many people also speak English

Must-see attractions: Ptuj Castle, Ptuj City Museum, Orpheus Monument, Ptuj Thermal Spa, Ptuj Wine Cellar

Triglav National Park:

Address: Julian Alps, Slovenia
Currency: Euro (EUR)
Language: Slovenian, but many people also speak English
Must-see attractions: Vintgar Gorge, Tolmin Gorges, Kozjak Waterfall, Lake Bohinj, Lake Bled, Triglav, Savica Waterfall

Lake Bohinj:

Address: Bohinj, Slovenia
Currency: Euro (EUR)
Language: Slovenian, but many people also speak English

Must-see attractions: Vogel Ski Resort, Savica Waterfall, Mount Triglav, Lake Bohinj, Mostnica Gorge, Church of St John the Baptist

Postojna Cave:

Address: Postojna, Slovenia
Currency: Euro (EUR)
Language: Slovenian, but many people also speak English

Must-see attractions: Postojna Cave, Predjama Castle, Expo Cave

Accommodations in Slovenia

Slovenia is a well-liked tourist destination renowned for its scenic surroundings, rich culture, and outdoor activities. The nation has a variety of lodging options, including hotels, hostels, guesthouses, and flats, to meet the demands of various traveller types.

In Slovenia, hotels are the most often used form of lodging, and they come in a variety of price points. The capital city of Ljubljana, as well as well-known tourist locations like Bled, Portoroz, and Piran, both, have a lot of hotels. The Grand Hotel Toplice in Bled, the Hotel Intercontinental in Ljubljana, and the Kempinski Palace Portoroz in Portoroz are a few well-known hotels in Slovenia.

For travellers on a tight budget, hostels are a popular option; many of them are found in well-known towns and tourist hotspots. Typically, hostels provide both private rooms and dorm-style lodging. The Youth Hostel Piran in Piran and the Celica Art Hostel in Ljubljana are two well-known hostels in Slovenia.

Another well-liked choice is staying at a guesthouse, especially for those seeking a more individualised experience. Guesthouses frequently offer breakfast and typically offer rooms in private residences or smaller hotels. The Guesthouse Pri Martinu in Ljubljana and the Pension Berc in Bled are two well-known inns in Slovenia.

Apartments are a popular option for tourists who value the privacy and flexibility of their place. There are rental alternatives for apartments in popular tourist areas and big towns, ranging from studio flats to bigger apartments fit for families or groups. Slovenians frequently use Airbnb to find houses and other types of vacation rentals.

Overall, Slovenia provides a variety of lodging options to meet the requirements of various travellers kinds and price ranges. There are many choices to make your stay in Slovenia comfortable and pleasurable, whether you're looking for a five-star hotel or a cheap hostel.

There are numerous ways for tourists and travellers to obtain lodging in Slovenia. Among the most well-liked techniques are:

Online travel agencies:

Numerous Internet travel agencies provide a variety of lodging options in Slovenia, including hotels, hostels, guesthouses, and flats. Expedia, Airbnb, and Booking.com are a few examples of well-known websites. Travellers can use these websites to compare prices, read testimonials from past visitors, and make online hotel reservations.

Information desks for travellers:

There are tourist information offices spread around Slovenia's major cities and tourist locations. These facilities provide a variety of services to visitors, such as directions, maps, and help with lodging reservations. A wide variety of brochures and flyers for local hotels, hostels, and guesthouses are also available at many tourist information centres.

Travel companies:

Travel agencies can also help tourists make hotel reservations in Slovenia. These organisations provide a variety of services, such as unique vacation plans, travel arrangements, and lodging. Travel agencies frequently have better negotiating power when it comes to hotel costs and occasionally provide package deals that include flights, lodging, and activities.

It's critical to take location, amenities, and cost into account when looking for lodging in Slovenia. Ljubljana, Bled, Portoroz, and Piran are a few of the well-liked places to stay in Slovenia. These locations provide a variety of lodging options and are close to well-liked activities and attractions.

The amenities that are vital to you should also be taken into account, such as free Wi-Fi, breakfast, air conditioning, and parking. To get a sense of the calibre of the lodgings and the level of service offered, read the evaluations left by past visitors.

Finally, if you're travelling during a busy period, make sure to reserve your lodging far in advance. Slovenia is a well-liked tourist destination, so hotels might get booked up quickly in the summer. You might get better deals and more selections when you reserve your accommodations in advance.

Addresses for some of the places and hotels mentioned above:

Grand Hotel Toplice in Bled: Cesta svobode 12, 4260 Bled, Slovenia

Hotel Intercontinental in Ljubljana: Slovenska cesta 59, 1000 Ljubljana, Slovenia

Kempinski Palace Portoroz in Portoroz: Obala 45, 6320 Portoroz, Slovenia

Celica Art Hostel in Ljubljana: Metelkova ulica 8, 1000 Ljubljana, Slovenia

Youth Hostel Piran in Piran: Gregorčičeva ulica 38, 6330 Piran, Slovenia

Guesthouse Pri Martinu in Ljubljana: Trubarjeva cesta 7, 1000 Ljubljana, Slovenia

Pension Berc in Bled: Ljubljanska cesta 5, 4260 Bled, Slovenia

For up-to-date pricing information, I would recommend visiting the websites of the individual hotels or booking websites mentioned earlier. You can also contact them directly for more information about their rates and availability.

Must-See Attractions in Slovenia

Slovenia is a small but incredibly beautiful country in Central Europe, known for its stunning natural landscapes, rich cultural heritage, and delicious cuisine.

Here are some must-see attractions for travellers and tourists visiting Slovenia:

Lake Bled: This iconic lake, with its picture-perfect island and castle, is one of Slovenia's top attractions. Visitors can take a traditional pletna boat to the island, explore the castle, and enjoy breathtaking views of the Julian Alps.

Postojna Cave: The Postojna Cave is one of the largest and most beautiful caves in Europe, with stunning rock formations, underground rivers, and unique wildlife. Visitors can take a train ride through the cave system and learn about its geological and biological history.

Ljubljana: Slovenia's capital city is a charming and vibrant destination, with a picturesque old town, stunning architecture, and a vibrant food and wine scene. Don't miss the iconic Triple Bridge and the Ljubljana Castle, which offers panoramic views of the city.

Piran: This beautiful coastal town on the Adriatic Sea is known for its Venetian architecture, narrow streets, and charming squares. Visitors can explore the old town, relax on the beach, and enjoy fresh seafood and local wines.

Triglav National Park: This stunning national park, located in the Julian Alps, is a paradise for nature lovers, with pristine lakes, waterfalls, and hiking trails. The park's highest peak, Mount Triglav, is a popular destination for experienced hikers and climbers.

Skocjan Caves: Another spectacular cave system in Slovenia, the Skocjan Caves are a UNESCO World Heritage Site, known for their enormous underground caverns, subterranean rivers, and unique geological formations.

Ptuj Castle: This beautiful medieval castle, located in the town of Ptuj, is one of Slovenia's best-preserved castles, with stunning views of the town and surrounding countryside. Visitors can explore the castle's history and enjoy cultural events and festivals throughout the year.

Soča Valley: This stunning alpine valley, known for its emerald-green river and dramatic mountain scenery, is a popular destination for outdoor activities such as hiking, rafting, and skiing.

Note: You can find pictures of each place mentioned in the possible itinerary.

These are just a few of the many must-see attractions in Slovenia. Whether you're interested in history, culture, nature, or adventure, Slovenia has something for everyone.

Here are the addresses and directions to each of the must-see attractions mentioned in Slovenia:

Lake Bled: Bled 4260, Slovenia. Visitors can take a bus or train to Bled and then walk to the lake, which is located in the town centre.

Postojna Cave: Jamska cesta 30, Postojna 6230, Slovenia. Visitors can take a train or bus to Postojna and then walk to the cave, which is located just outside of town.

Ljubljana: Visitors can fly into Ljubljana Jože Pučnik Airport or take a train or bus to the city centre. The main attractions, such as the Triple Bridge and Ljubljana Castle, are within walking distance of each other.

Piran: Tartinijev trg 1, Piran 6330, Slovenia. Visitors can take a bus or taxi to Piran or drive themselves. The town centre is pedestrian-only, so visitors must park outside the town and walk in.

Triglav National Park: Visitors can enter the park at various locations, such as Bled or Bohinj. Hiking trails and attractions within the park are accessible by foot or by car.

Skocjan Caves: Matavun 12, Divača 6215, Slovenia. Visitors can take a train or bus to Divača and then walk to the cave, which is located just outside of town.

Ptuj Castle: Muzejski trg 1, Ptuj 2250, Slovenia. Visitors can take a bus or train to Ptuj and then walk to the castle, which is located in the town centre.

Soča Valley: Visitors can access the valley from various towns, such as Bovec or Kobarid. Hiking trails and attractions within the valley are accessible by foot or by car.

It's worth noting that Slovenia is a small country with a well-developed public transportation system, so it's easy to get around by bus or train. Taxis and rental cars are also available for those who prefer more flexibility.

Off the Beaten Path: Hidden Gems in Slovenia

Slovenia is a stunning nation with a deep cultural heritage. While many visitors may be drawn to Slovenia's well-known locations, such as Lake Bled or the capital city of Ljubljana, many undiscovered jewels are well worth discovering.

Here are some unusual locations for tourists and travellers to explore:

Piran:

The Adriatic Sea is home to this little coastal town, which is renowned for its tiny, twisting alleys and Venetian-style buildings. The village is a wonderful spot to unwind and savour some fresh seafood and offers breathtaking views of the sea and the hills surrounding it.

Skocjan Caves::

One of the world's largest underground canyons, the Skocjan Caves are a UNESCO World Heritage site. The amazing formations and underground river can be seen when on a guided tour inside the caverns.

Logar Valley:

The Kamnik-Savinja Alps' scenic valley, which provides breathtaking views of the neighbouring mountains, waterfalls, and meadows, is situated there. In the winter, it is a fantastic location for skiing, riding, and hiking.

Kobarid:

This little town in Slovenia's western region is well-known for its involvement in World War I. The town's museum is open for visitors to explore, where they can find out more about the local wars. The village makes a fantastic starting point for mountain hikes nearby.

Predjama Castle:

One of the most unusual and beautiful castles in all of Europe, this mediaeval fortress was carved into the cliff's side. Visitors can tour the castle's numerous rooms and discover its extensive history.

Lake Bohinj:

Although Lake Bled may be the more well-known attraction, Lake Bohinj is equally lovely and less crowded. The Julian Alps around the lake, which provides breathtaking views of the peaks and the glistening water.

Idrija:

The second-largest mercury mine in the world is located in this little town, which has a long history of mining. The mMiningseumis open to anyone who wants to learn more about the region's mining heritage.

Overall, Slovenia is a nation that is full of undiscovered jewels waiting to be found. There is something in this magnificent nation for everyone, whether you enjoy history, the outdoors, or just unwinding in a picturesque environment.

Off the Beaten Path: Hidden Gems in Slovenia

Slovenia is a magnificent nation in Central Europe that is well-known for its lovely natural surroundings, quaint towns and cities, and extensive cultural history. While many visitors visit well-known locations like Ljubljana, Bled, and Piran, there are numerous undiscovered jewels just waiting to be found by those prepared to stray from the way less travelled.

Here are some ideas for visitors and travellers who desire to discover Slovenia's undiscovered attractions:

Idrija:

Idrija, a charming village in western Slovenia, is well-known for having a mercury mine that operated for more than 500 years. The Idrija Municipal Museum offers mine tours and information on the town's mining history. Additionally, the town includes a wonderful historic district with Baroque structures, little lanes, and a castle.

Kobarid:

Outdoor enthusiasts love to visit this little town in the Julian Alps because it offers trails for biking, hiking, and water sports. The Kobarid Museum, which depicts the tale of the local World

War I battlefields, is also located in Kobarid.

Škocjan Caves:

The Kocjan Caves are a lesser-known but no less stunning natural marvel in Slovenia than the Postojna Caves, which are a well-liked tourist destination. A vast subterranean canyon, waterfalls, and unusual rock formations can be seen in the caves, which are UNESCO World Heritage Sites.

Ptuj:

Ptuj, a town in northeastern Slovenia, is among the oldest in the nation and has been inhabited since the Roman era. The town contains a historical district with well-preserved mediaeval and

Baroque structures, a castle, and a hot spa.

Logar Valley:

With routes leading to waterfalls, alpine meadows, and mountain summits, this magnificent valley in the Kamnik-Savinja Alps is a hiker and nature enthusiast's dream come true. Traditional wooden farmhouses and a small museum that highlights the way of life in the area may also be found in the valley.

Vipava Valley:

This Slovenian wine area in the southwest is renowned for its lovely landscape, quaint towns, and top-notch wines. Visitors are welcome to tour the vineyards, taste the local wines, and dine on regional specialities at nearby eateries.

Lipica Stud Farm:

The renowned Lipizzaner horses, which are bred for classical dressage, are kept at this storied stud farm close to the Slovenian-Italian border. Visitors may take a farm tour, see how the horses are trained, and even ride in a carriage.

Velika Planina:

The Kamnik-Savinja Alps' high alpine plateau is a special place with old-fashioned wooden shepherd houses and breathtaking views of the neighbouring mountains. To get to the plateau, tourists may climb or use a cable car. Once there, they can explore the hiking paths that lead to alpine meadows, picturesque vistas, and a small museum about the way of life in the area.

Radovljica:

Tourists often skip over this little village next to Bled, yet it has a lot to offer. The town's historic district has a castle and well-preserved mediaeval structures.

The Museum of Apiculture offers visitors the opportunity to learn about beekeeping, which is another tradition in Radovljica.

Tolmin Gorge:

This western Slovenian natural marvel has waterfalls, ponds, and a small ravine with crystal-pure water. On wooden stairways and bridges, visitors may trek into the gorge while taking in the breathtaking surroundings.

Solčavsko:

Located in the eastern Kamnik-Savinja Alps, this secluded area is a hidden treasure with beautiful scenery, historic buildings, and rich cultural history. Visitors may stroll through nearby towns, climb picturesque vistas, and visit the Solavsko Museum to discover the culture and history of the area.

Žiče Charterhouse:

This hidden treasure has a rich history; it is a mediaeval monastery close to Slovenske Konjice. The monastery was established in the 12th century and was significant to the area's ecclesiastical and cultural life. The chapel, library, and cloister of the monastery are open to visitors who want to learn more about the monks who formerly resided there.

These are just a handful of the many undiscovered beauties in Slovenia. Whether you're a seasoned tourist or a first-time visitor, seeing Slovenia's lesser-known locales will allow you to have a memorable and genuine experience of this beautiful nation.

Experiencing the Local Culture in Slovenia

There are numerous methods for visitors and travellers to explore and immerse themselves in the local culture of Slovenia, a nation rich in culture and history.

Here are a few ideas:

Explore Ljubljana:

Slovenia's capital city is a centre for artistic endeavours, with theatres, galleries, and museums. Walking around the city centre is simple since it is designed for pedestrians. Traditional Slovenian food may be found in a variety of cafés and restaurants, and tourists can take advantage of festivals and live entertainment all year long.

Explore the countryside:

Slovenia's landscape is dotted with charming towns and villages, many of which still follow a traditional way of life. Visitors may choose to go on a guided tour or hire a vehicle and go exploring on their own while admiring the breathtaking surroundings and discovering the customs and traditions of the area.

Attend a festival:

With a full schedule of festivals and events throughout the year, Slovenia boasts a vibrant cultural scene. These include the Bled Days Festival, the Ljubljana Jazz Festival, and the Kurentovanje Festival, which celebrates the arrival of spring with vibrant costumes and folk music.

Typical local fare and beverage:

Visitors may try traditional meals such as poetic (a sweet breadKranjskaska kilobase (a sausage), and a dove ganci (buckwheat porridge), which are influenced by Austrian, Italian, and Balkan cultures. There are a variety of regional wines and beers to sample as well, including the dark beer from the Pivovarna Union brewery and the delicious white wine of the Brda area.

Visit galleries and museums:

To fully appreciate Slovenia's rich cultural legacy, tourists should visit its museums and art galleries. The National Museum of Slovenia, the Museum of Modern Art in Ljubljana, and the Idrija Municipal Museum, which highlights the area's extensive mining heritage, are a few illustrious establishments.

Historical locations to visit

There are several historical monuments, such as castles, cathedrals, and prehistoric ruins, to visit in Slovenia because of its extensive past. The Predjama Castle, a 13th-century fortress built into a cliff, the Postojna Cave, a unique underground world with a vast cave system, and the Kocjan Caves, UNESCO World Heritage sites with a magnificent underground canyon, are a few of the most well-known attractions.

Participate in outdoor pursuits:

Slovenia is renowned for its outdoor pursuits, including water sports, skiing, cycling, and hiking. Visitors may experience the local culture via outdoor excursions while seeing the nation's breathtaking natural features, such as the Julian Alps, Triglav National Park, and Lake Bled.

Stay at a conventional hotel:

Visitors may stay in conventional lodgings including farm stays, guesthouses, and eco-friendly lodges to get a true sense of the local culture. These lodgings provide a window into local culture and provide an opportunity to discover local crafts, agriculture, and food.

Visit a neighbourhood market:

Slovenia has a thriving market culture, and many of its villages and cities have weekly or daily markets where tourists may purchase local goods including fresh vegetables, handicrafts, and trinkets. In Ljubljana, the Central Market is especially well-known and offers a variety of items, including regional cheese, honey, and dried fruit.

Pick up the language:

Finally, gaining a basic understanding of Slovenian might help one better integrate within the community. Visitors who attempt to speak in the local tongue are appreciated by the community, and it may also improve the whole trip experience by fostering more meaningful encounters and relationships.

In conclusion, there are a variety of opportunities for visitors and travellers to experience the local culture in Slovenia, including visiting historical sites and museums, trying local cuisine and beverages, and engaging in outdoor sports. Visitors may get a greater understanding of Slovenia's rich history and customs and create lifelong memories by being fully immersed in the local culture.

Outdoor Activities in Slovenia

Slovenia offers a variety of year-round outdoor and cultural experiences, but the ideal time to go depends on personal tastes and interests.

For instance, the summer season (June to August) offers great weather for outdoor pursuits like biking, hiking, and water sports, as well as several festivals and events. It's a terrific time of year to explore the countryside and attend local markets since the weather is often pleasant and bright.

For those who prefer hiking and sightseeing, autumn (September to November) is a fantastic season to travel since the autumn foliage provides a beautiful background for outdoor activities. Additionally, a lot of regional harvest celebrations take place around this time, when guests may indulge in regional food.

For those who prefer winter activities like skiing and snowboarding, the winter season (December to February) is great, and the Christmas markets in Ljubljana and other cities create a joyful mood. Due to the lower number of visitors, winter may also be a fantastic season to visit historical monuments and museums.

For those interested in attending cultural events and festivals like the Kurentovanje Festival and the Ljubljana Jazz Festival, spring (March to May) is a fantastic time to go. It's a terrific time to go outside since it's pleasant outside and the countryside is beginning to blossom.

In conclusion, there are numerous times of the year to enjoy Slovenia's varied cultural and outdoor activities, and travellers should take their interests and preferences into account when choosing when to go.

It's also important to keep in mind that Slovenia's peak travel season typically lasts from June through September, with July and August being the busiest months. Popular locations like Lake Bled and the seaside may become fairly busy during this season, and costs for lodging and entertainment may be higher than they are at other times of the year.

On the other side, travelling in the off-peak months of April through May and September through October may provide a more laid-back and budget-friendly experience with fewer tourists and milder weather. For those interested in winter sports or cultural events, winter may also be a terrific season to travel, but it's vital to keep in mind that certain sights and activities can be closed during this time.

The ideal time to visit Slovenia ultimately relies on personal choices and interests. It's usually a good idea to investigate the weather, occasions, and seasonal activities in the places you want to visit and, if at all feasible, reserve lodging and activities in advance, particularly during the busiest times of the year. No matter when a person decides to come, Slovenia has much to offer them thanks to its rich cultural legacy and breathtaking natural beauty.

Museums and galleries in Slovenia

Slovenia has a rich cultural heritage, and there are many museums and galleries throughout the country that offer a glimpse into its history and art.

Here are some of the top museums and galleries in Slovenia that travellers and tourists may want to visit:

National Museum of Slovenia:

This museum in Ljubljana is the oldest and largest museum in Slovenia, featuring archaeological, historical, and artistic collections.

Museum of Contemporary Art Metelkova (MSUM):

Located in Ljubljana's Metelkova neighbourhood, MSUM is a contemporary art museum that showcases works from both Slovenian and international artists.

National Gallery of Slovenia:

The National Gallery of Slovenia, also located in Ljubljana, is the country's main art museum, featuring a collection of Slovenian art from the medieval period to the present day.

Museum of Illusions:

This museum in Ljubljana is a fun and interactive experience for visitors of all ages, featuring optical illusions and exhibits that challenge your perception.

Ptuj Castle:

Ptuj Castle in northeastern Slovenia is home to several museums, including the Ptuj Regional Museum, which features exhibits on the history and culture of the Ptuj region.

Slovenian Alpine Museum:

Located in Mojstrana, the Slovenian Alpine Museum is dedicated to the history and culture of mountaineering in Slovenia.

Kobarid Museum:

This museum in Kobarid is dedicated to the history of World War I in Slovenia and features exhibits on the battles that took place in the region.

Lipizzaner Museum Lipica:

This museum in Lipica is dedicated to the famous Lipizzaner horses, which have been bred in Slovenia for over 400 years.

Božidar Jakac Art Museum:

The Božidar Jakac Art Museum in Kostanjevica na Krki features works by the Slovenian painter Božidar Jakac, as well as other Slovenian and international artists.

These are just a few examples of the many museums and galleries in Slovenia that travellers and tourists may want to visit. Each museum offers a unique insight into Slovenia's history, culture, and art, and can make for an enriching and educational experience.

Here are the addresses and brief instructions on how to locate each of the museums and galleries mentioned earlier:

National Museum of Slovenia: Prešernova cesta 20, 1000 Ljubljana, Slovenia. The museum is located in the centre of Ljubljana, near the Triple Bridge and the Ljubljana Castle.

Museum of Contemporary Art Metelkova (MSUM): Maistrova ulica 3, 1000 Ljubljana, Slovenia. The museum is located in the Metelkova neighbourhood, which is a short walk from the main train station.

National Gallery of Slovenia: Prešernova cesta 24, 1000 Ljubljana, Slovenia. The museum is located in the centre of Ljubljana, near the National Museum of Slovenia.

Museum of Illusions: Kongresni trg 14, 1000 Ljubljana, Slovenia. The museum is located in the heart of Ljubljana, near the Slovenian Philharmonic and the Town Hall.

Ptuj Castle: Muzejski trg 1, 2250 Ptuj, Slovenia. The castle is located in the town of Ptuj, which is about a 1.5-hour drive northeast of Ljubljana.

Slovenian Alpine Museum: Triglavska cesta 49, 4281 Mojstrana, Slovenia. The museum is located in the town of

Mojstrana, which is about a 45-minute drive northwest of Ljubljana.

Kobarid Museum: Trg svobode 16, 5222 Kobarid, Slovenia. The museum is located in the town of Kobarid, which is about a 2-hour drive west of Ljubljana.

Lipizzaner Museum Lipica: Lipica 5, 6210 Sežana, Slovenia. The museum is located in the town of Lipica, which is about a 1-hour drive southwest of Ljubljana.

Božidar Jakac Art Museum: Grajska cesta 3, 8311 Kostanjevica na Krki, Slovenia. The museum is located in the town of Kostanjevica na Krki, which is about a 1-hour drive southeast of Ljubljana.

I hope this helps you locate these museums and galleries in Slovenia. Enjoy your visit!

Food and Drink in Slovenia

Slovenia has a diverse culinary scene that combines elements of Central

European, Mediterranean, and Balkan cuisines.

Here are some must-try foods and drinks for travellers and tourists visiting Slovenia:

Carniolan Sausage (Kranjska kilobase):

This is a traditional Slovenian sausage made from pork meat and bacon, flavoured with garlic and smoked over beechwood. It's often served with sauerkraut or mustard.

Bled Cream Cake (Kremna retina):

A delicious cake made of layers of puff pastry filled with vanilla cream and topped with whipped cream and powdered sugar. It's named after the picturesque town of Bled, where it originated.

Potica:

A sweet and nutty cake roll made from yeast dough, filled with various fillings such as walnuts, poppy seeds, tarragon, or chocolate.

Slovenian Wine:

Slovenia has a long tradition of winemaking, and its wine regions produce excellent white and red wines. Some popular varieties include Rebula, Malvasia, and Cviček.

Beer:

Slovenia also has a growing craft beer scene, with many microbreweries producing unique and tasty brews. Some popular brands include HumanFish, Pelicon, and Reservoir Dogs.

Štruklji:

These are traditional Slovenian dumplings made of dough and filled with various ingredients, such as cottage cheese, nuts, or apples. They can be served as a main dish or a dessert.

Idrija Žlikrofi:

A type of pasta similar to Italian gnocchi, filled with potato and bacon. It's a speciality of the town of Idrija.

Prekmurska gibanica:

A delicious layered pastry made with poppy seeds, apples, walnuts, and cottage cheese. It's a traditional dessert from the Prekmurje region in northeastern Slovenia.

Herbal liqueurs:

Slovenia is known for its herbal liqueurs, such as Borovniček (blueberry liqueur), Medica (honey liqueur), and Pelinkovac (wormwood liqueur).

Laško and Union Beer:

These are two of the most popular beer brands in Slovenia, and you can find them in almost every pub or restaurant. They are both light lagers and are perfect for pairing with traditional Slovenian dishes.

In conclusion, Slovenia offers a diverse culinary scene with a unique blend of Central European, Mediterranean, and Balkan cuisines. Tourists and travellers visiting Slovenia should try traditional dishes such as Carniolan Sausage, Bled Cream Cake, Potica, Štruklji, Idrija Žlikrofi, and Prekmurska gibanica. They should also sample Slovenian wine, craft beer, and herbal liqueurs such as Borovniček, Medica, and Pelinkovac.

As for locations and addresses where these foods and drinks can be found, they can be easily found throughout Slovenia, from local markets and street vendors to high-end restaurants and bars.

Here are some popular locations and addresses where tourists and travellers can try these dishes:

Carniolan Sausage: can be found in most restaurants throughout Slovenia, especially in Ljubljana's Central Market, which is open daily.

Bled Cream Cake: can be found at the famous Hotel Park in Bled or any pastry shop in Slovenia.

Potica: can be found at any bakery or pastry shop in Slovenia, especially in the Prekmurje region.

Slovenian Wine: can be sampled at any of the country's wine regions, such as Goriška Brda or Podravje.

Beer: can be found in many pubs and microbreweries throughout Slovenia, such as Union Brewery in Ljubljana.

Štruklji: can be found in traditional Slovenian restaurants such as Gostilna As in Ljubljana or Gostilna Pri Danilu in Idrija.

Idrija Žlikrofi: can be found at restaurants in the Idrija region, such as Gostilna Žlikrofi or Jožica's Kitchen.

Prekmurska gibanica: can be found at any bakery or pastry shop in the Prekmurje region.

Herbal liqueurs: can be found in most bars and liquor stores throughout Slovenia, such as the Café Bar Tempo in Ljubljana or the Tržaška Kavarna in Maribor.

Overall, visitors to Slovenia will find a wide range of delicious and unique food and drink options to explore and enjoy.

Campsites in Slovenia that offer facilities for RVs

Slovenia has a large number of campgrounds with amenities for recreational vehicles. Here are a few possibilities:

Campsite Adria:

This campground, which is situated in Ankaran on the Adriatic coast, provides 430 RV pitches. There are amenities including electricity, water, trash removal, restrooms, and a restaurant.

Campsite Bled:

This campground offers 250 RV spaces beside Lake Bled. There are amenities including electricity, water, trash removal, showers, lavatories, and a grocery store.

Campsite Terme Čatež:

This campground, which is situated in the community of Ate ob Savi, provides 430 RV spots. Facilities include access to the neighbouring thermal spa as well as electricity, water, garbage disposal, showers, and WCs.

Park Lijak Campground:

This campground, which is situated in the village of Ozeljan, provides 80 RV spots. There are amenities including electricity, water, trash removal, restrooms, and a restaurant. A paragliding centre is also not far from the campsite.

Campsite Sobec:

This campground, which is close to the town of Bled, provides 400 RV sites. There are amenities including electricity, water, trash removal, showers, lavatories, and a grocery store. The Sava Dolinka River, which provides options for rafting and kayaking, is also adjacent to the campsite.

These are only a few of the several campgrounds in Slovenia that provide amenities for RVs. By conducting an online search or consulting a camping handbook, you can locate more possibilities.

A broad overview of Slovenian camping costs.

In Slovenia, the cost of a normal pitch with the most basic amenities (electricity, water, trash disposal, showers, and toilets) typically ranges from 10 to 30 euros per night. The location, pitch size, and season will all affect the final cost.

Additionally, some campgrounds may charge extra for extras like WiFi access, sports facilities, or swimming pools. To find out the most recent rates, it's usually a good idea to visit the specific campground's website or get in touch with them.

It's also important to keep in mind that some campgrounds may provide savings for extended stays, group reservations, or off-peak times.

Shopping in Slovenia

Slovenia is a lovely nation that provides visitors and travellers with a distinctive shopping experience. The nation is renowned for its fine handmade goods, which include lacework, ceramics, wooden crafts, glassware, and honey.

Here are a few of Slovenia's well-liked shopping areas:

Ljubljana:

The Slovenian capital city offers a wide range of shopping possibilities, from upscale luxury boutiques to little craft outlets. The Old Town is a well-liked place to go shopping, particularly for trinkets, crafts, and regional specialties.

Piran:

Visitors must purchase some of the traditional lacework from Piran, a coastal village. Numerous stores in the village also sell handmade jewellery, ceramics, and olive oil.

Bled:

Bled, a popular tourist destination, is known for its magnificent lake and castle, but it also provides a distinctive shopping experience. Visitors can buy honey, hand-painted pottery, and wooden toys manufactured in the area.

Maribor:

The second-largest city in Slovenia features a selection of high-street shops and retail malls. The Lent Market, which takes place in December and features a variety of homemade presents, decorations, and regional specialties, is the city's main draw.

Bohinj:

For outdoor enthusiasts, Bohinj is a charming town that is a top choice. Visitors can buy locally produced cheese and honey, as well as handcrafted wool items like hats and gloves.

Overall, shopping in Slovenia gives visitors and travellers a chance to learn about the distinctive culture and traditions of the nation. High-quality handmade items can be purchased by tourists as wonderful mementos or presents for loved ones.

Health and Safety in Slovenia

The majority of the time, tourists and travellers may feel secure in Slovenia. To preserve your health and safety while travelling, it is crucial to always take precautions.

Here are a few advices:

COVID-19:

In light of the ongoing COVID-19 pandemic, it's critical to be informed about the most recent Slovenian travel restrictions and recommendations. It is advisable to confirm these before travelling with the Slovenian embassy or consulate in your country as they may change often.

Health Care:

Slovenia has an advanced healthcare system, and there are hospitals both public and private all around the nation. However, because medical expenses can be significant, it is advised to carry travel insurance that covers medical emergencies and evacuation.

Water:

There is no need to purchase bottled water in Slovenia because the tap water is safe to consume.

Crime:

Slovenia generally has low crime rates and is a safe country. However, it is always advisable to exercise caution and pay attention to your surroundings, particularly in major cities or tourist hotspots where theft and pickpocketing are possible occurrences.

Natural catastrophes:

If you're travelling to Slovenia, it's a good idea to prepare for earthquakes because the country is in an earthquake-prone area. The Slovenian government provides details on earthquake protection precautions and protocols.

Outdoor activities:

Slovenia offers a lot of options for outdoor enthusiasts to engage in sports like hiking, skiing, and other outdoor pursuits. But it's crucial to take the proper safety precautions, like checking the weather before you start your activity and donning the right clothing.

Traffic:

Although Slovenia's roads are well-maintained, it is nevertheless vital to drive defensively and follow all traffic regulations, particularly on twisting mountain roads.

In conclusion, Slovenia is a safe travel and tourism destination, but it is always advisable to exercise caution and be ready for anything.

Tips for Traveling in Slovenia on a Budget

Slovenia is a stunning nation with stunning landscapes, quaint cities, and a rich cultural history.

Here are some pointers for tourists and travellers who want to see Slovenia on a tight budget:

Visit during the shoulder season:

Slovenia's peak tourism period is from June to August, so if you can go between April and May or September and October, you may avoid the crowds and save money on lodging.

Take the bus or train:

Slovenia's public transport network, which includes buses and railroads, is highly developed. You may save a lot of money by taking the bus or train instead of renting a car, and it's a terrific way to see the country.

Use hostels or low-cost hotels:

Hostels and low-cost hotels are only a couple of the affordable lodging choices available in Slovenia. It is simple to walk around the city because these are frequently found in strategic locations.

Consume locally:

You may discover wonderful local food at reasonable costs in Slovenia, which has a strong culinary culture. Look for local markets and food carts, and try meals like evapii, burek, or kremna rezina that are considered traditional.

Explore the outdoors:

Many of the best outdoor activities in Slovenia, which is renowned for its breathtaking natural beauty, are either free or inexpensive. There are many free ways to enjoy the outdoors, including hiking, riding, and swimming in lakes or natural pools.

Benefit from free activities:

In Slovenia, several museums, art galleries, and other cultural institutions grant free entrance, particularly on particular days of the week or during particular exhibitions. For more details, check out their websites or the local directories.

Plan ahead:

You may cut costs on travel, lodging, and activities by completing your homework and making plans in advance. Look for deals on bus and train tickets, reserve lodging in advance, and design your itinerary to take advantage of activities that are free or inexpensive.

Take a look at a city tourism card:

Tourist cards with discounts on attractions, public transport and other services are available in several Slovenian cities. These cards might help you arrange your trip more easily and for less money.

Visit villages and smaller towns:

Although Ljubljana and Bled are well-known tourist sites, Slovenia's smaller towns and villages can provide a more genuine experience at a lesser cost. Think about going to destinations like Kofja Loka, Kranj, or Piran.

Drink tap water:

Slovenia's tap water is safe to drink, so you may save money and lessen the amount of plastic waste by avoiding buying bottled water.

Use unpaid Wi-Fi:

Slovenia has a large number of establishments that provide free Wi-Fi, so there's no need to pay for data or international roaming fees.

Reserve tours and activities ahead of time:

When you reserve in advance for a guided activity or trip, you can frequently save money. Search for savings on sites like Viator or GetYourGuide, or reserve tickets directly from neighbourhood tour guides.

Slovenia offers a variety of inexpensive lodging, dining, and activities, making it a fantastic choice for tourists on a budget. You may have an amazing trip without going overboard if you prepare in advance and use available resources in your area.

Conclusion: Making the Most of Your Trip to Slovenia

Slovenia is a stunning country with a wealth of tourist sites and activities to offer. Slovenia has much to offer everyone, whether they want to discover the country's natural beauty, cultural legacy, or energetic cities.

Plan early and do your homework on the places you want to see to make the most of your vacation to Slovenia. The Julian Alps, Lake Bled, the Postojna Cave, and Slovenia's capital city Ljubljana are a few of the country's prominent tourist destinations.

Respecting Slovenia's culture and traditions is essential when travelling there. Slovenians are very hospitable to guests and proud of their culture. To make your trip even more enjoyable, try some of the local cuisine and pick up some Slovenian.

Slovenia has a wide variety of outdoor activities to choose from. There are numerous paths and parks to explore, and the sports like hiking, skiing, cycling, and kayaking are very popular here.

Slovenia offers a distinctive fusion of natural beauty, cultural legacy, and outdoor activities, making it a superb travel and tourist destination overall. You may make the most of your trip and have a wonderful experience in this beautiful country with a little preparation and research.

Slovenia's weather should be taken into account as well when travelling there. With pleasant summers and chilly winters, Slovenia's temperature is typically mild, though it might vary depending on the place you're visiting. It's crucial to check the weather forecast in advance if you're planning any outdoor activities to make sure the weather will be favourable.

Slovenia's train and bus networks are well connected, and there are vehicle rental services available, making transportation there also quite simple. Due to the tiny roads and rocky terrain, driving in Slovenia can be difficult, therefore it's vital to exercise caution and be familiar with the local traffic laws.

There are numerous festivals and events hosted all year long if you're interested in Slovenian culture, including the Ljubljana Festival, the Lent Festival, and the Maribor Festival. These celebrations offer a wonderful chance to become immersed in the community's culture while showcasing Slovenian music, dancing, and cuisine.

Finally, when visiting Slovenia, it's critical to keep the environment in mind. The nation's natural beauty is renowned, and it must be protected for coming generations. Respect wildlife and vegetation, adhere to the principles of Leave No Trace, and refrain from littering or causing harm to natural areas.

In conclusion, Slovenia is a superb vacation and tourist destination for those seeking a distinctive fusion of the outdoors, cultural legacy, and natural beauty. You can have an unforgettable experience in this magnificent country if you plan well, have an open mind, and are willing to explore.